Saru

To Grace, who knew
Owl could count.
—S.M.

Copyright © 2000 by Suse MacDonald.
All rights reserved. Published by Scholastic Inc.
SCHOLASTIC, CARTWHEEL BOOKS and associated logos
are trademarks and/or registered trademarks of Scholastic Inc.

Library of Congress Cataloging-in-Publication Data available

ISBN 0-590-68320-9

10 9 8 7 6 5 4 3 2 1   00 01 02 03 04

Printed in Mexico   49
First printing, October 2000

LOOK WHOOO'S COUNTING

Suse MacDonald

SCHOLASTIC INC.

New York   Toronto   London   Auckland   Sydney
Mexico City   New Delhi   Hong Kong

When Owl was young,
she could not count.

Flying through the sky one night,
she learned.

Owl saw **1** prairie dog on a hill.

She counted 1.

Owl saw 2 mice in the field.

She counted 1, 2.

Owl saw **3** ducks near the pond.

She counted 1, 2, 3.

Owl saw **4** moths in the grass.

She counted 1, 2, 3, 4.

Owl saw **5** cranes in the moonlight.

She counted 1, 2, 3, 4, 5.

Owl saw **6** big-horned sheep in the cliffs.

She counted 1, 2, 3, 4, 5, 6.

Owl saw **7** bats fly across the moon.

She counted 1, 2, 3, 4, 5, 6, 7.

Owl saw **8** spiders in a web.

She counted 1, 2, 3, 4, 5, 6, 7, 8.

Owl saw 9 squirrels in a tree.

She counted 1, 2, 3, 4, 5, 6, 7, 8, 9.

At dawn, Owl saw **10** snails among the flowers.

She counted 1, 2, 3, 4, 5, 6, 7, 8, 9, 10.

Count from 1 to 10 with wise old Owl.

6 7 8 9 10

Now look who's counting!